This Journal Belongs To:

. . . .

. . . .

. . . .

. . . .

To: Dr. Dhaliwal   From: Makayla

Thank you for being an amazing teacher I am the luckiest student ever hope you enjoy you're christmas break!

P.S.
thank you for everything you do for me!

To the world you may be just a teacher but to your students you are a HERO - Anonymous

A child educated only at school is an uneducated child.
- George Santayana

A child miseducated is a child lost.
- John F. Kennedy

A good education is like a savings account; the more you put
into it, the richer you are. - Victor Hugo

A good teacher can inspire hope
- Brad Henry

A good teacher is a good student first. By repeating his lessons, he acquires excellence.- M. K. Soni

A good teacher is a master of simplification and an enemy of simplism. -- Louis A. Berman

A good teacher is like a candle it consumes itself to light the way for others. - Mustafa Kemal Atatürk

A good teacher is one who makes himself progressively
unnecessary.- Thomas Carruthers

A man should first direct himself in the way he should go. Only then should he instruct others. ~ O'Bryan Brian

A master can tell you what he expects of you. A teacher, though, awakens your own expectations. ~ Patricia Neal

A talent is formed in stillness, a character in the world's torrent.
- Johann W. Goethe

A teacher affects eternity; he can never tell where his influence stops. -- Henry Brooks Adams

A teacher is a compass that activates the magnets of curiosity, knowledge, and wisdom in the pupils. -- Eve Garrison

A teacher is one who makes himself progressively unnecessary
-- Thomas Carruthers

A teacher should have maximal authority, and minimal power.
~Thomas Szasz

A teacher takes a hand, opens a mind, and touches a heart.
~John Cotton

A teacher's job is to take a bunch of live wires and see that they
are well-grounded. ~D. Martin

A true disciple shows his appreciation by reaching further than his teacher. - Aristotle

A truly special teacher is very wise, and sees tomorrow in every child's eyes. ~John Cotton

Acquire new knowledge whilst thinking over the old, and you may become a teacher of others. - Confucius

Always be a first-rate version of yourself, instead of a second-rate version of somebody else. -Judy Garland

An excellent plumber is infinitely more admirable than an incompetent philosopher. John W. Gardner

An object in possession seldom contains the same charm that it had in pursuit. - Pliny the Younger

Anyone who stops learning is old, whether at twenty or eighty.
Anyone who keeps learning stays young. - Henry Ford

Appreciation is a wonderful thing. It makes what is excellent in others belong to us as well. ~Voltaire

As a general rule, teachers teach more by what they are than by
what they say.~ Thurgood Marshall

Awaken people's curiosity. It is enough to open minds, do not overload them. Put there just a spark. - Anatole France

Be all that you can be. Find your future--as a teacher.
--Madeline Fuchs Holzer

Be an opener of doors for such as come after thee.
~ Ralph Waldo Emerson

Be the change you want to see in the world.
- Mahatma Gandhi

Being a new teacher is like trying to fly a plane while building it.
~ Rick Smith

Better than a thousand days of diligent study is one day with a great teacher.--Japanese proverb

Bitter are the roots of study, but how sweet their fruit.
- Cato

Blessed is the man who, having nothing to say, abstains from giving us wordy evidence of the fact. - George Eliot

Books let us into their souls and lay open to us the secrets of our own. -William Hazlitt

By learning you will teach; by teaching you will understand.
- Latin Proverb

Children learn more from what you are than what you teach.
-- W. E. B. DuBois

Come forth into the light of things, let nature be your teacher.
- William Wordsworth

Discover wildlife: be a teacher!
~John Cotton

Do not confine your children to your own learning, for they were
born in another time. - (Chinese Proverb)

Education breeds confidence. Confidence breeds hope. Hope
breeds peace. - (Confucius)

Education can be dangerous. It is very difficult to make it not dangerous. In fact, it is almost impossible.
- Robert M. Hutchins

Education is an ornament in prosperity and refuge in adversity.
-- Aristotle

Education is light, lack of it darkness.
--Russian proverb

Education is not preparation for life; education is life itself.
- John Dewey

Education is not the filling of a pail, but the lighting of a fire.
- William Butler Yeats

Education is the best provision for the journey to old age.
- Aristotle

Education is the mother of leadership.
- Wendell L. Willkie

Education is the transmission of civilization.
- Will Durant

Education is what most receive, many pass on, and few possess.
- Karl Kraus

Education should turn out the pupil with something he knows well and something he can do well. - Alfred North Whitehead

Education's purpose is to replace an empty mind with an open one. - Malcolm Forbes

Even the clearest water appears opaque at great depth.
-    *Victor Hugo*

Every artist was at first an amateur.
- Ralph W. Emerson

Everyone hears what you say. Friends listen to what you say.
Best friends listen to what you don't say. -Thurgood Marshall

Experience fails to teach where there is no desire to learn.
-- George Bernard Shaw

Experience is a dear teacher, but fools will learn at no other.
-- Benjamin Franklin

Experience is the worst teacher; it gives the test before presenting the lesson. - Vernon Law

Feeling gratitude and not expressing it is like wrapping a present and not giving it. ~William Arthur Ward

For every person who wants to teach there are approximately thirty people who don't want to learn much. ~ W.C. Stellar

From what we get, we can make a living; from what we give,
however, makes a life. -Arthur Ashe

Genius without education is like silver in the mine.
- Benjamin Franklin

Give me a fish and I eat for a day. Teach me to fish and I eat for a lifetime. ~ Chinese Proverb

Give me four years to teach the children and the seed I have sown will never be uprooted. - Vladimir Lenin

Good teachers are costly, but bad teachers cost more.
- Bob Talbert

Good teachers deserve apples; great teachers deserve chocolate.
- Richard Hamming

Good teaching is more a giving of right questions than a giving of right answers. - Josef Albers

Good teaching is one-fourth preparation and three-fourths pure
theatre. ~Gail Godwin

Great spirits have always encountered violent opposition from
mediocre minds. -Albert Einstein

Great spirits have always encountered violent opposition from mediocre minds. -Albert Einstein

He that teaches us anything which we knew not before is
undoubtedly to be reverenced as a master. - Samuel Johnson

He who dares to teach must never cease to learn.
~ Richard Henry Dann

"He who knows what best to omit is the best teacher.
— Otto Neurath"

He who opens a school door, closes a prison.
-    Victor Hugo

Human history becomes more and more a race between education and catastrophe. - HG Wells

I am a teacher. The only profession where you steal things from home and bring them to work. ~ Thurgood Marshall

I am indebted to my father for living, but to my teacher for living well. ~Alexander the Great

I am not a teacher, but an awakener.
- Robert Frost

I am not ashamed to confess that I am ignorant of what I do not know. - Marcus T. Cicero

I am not just a teacher, I am the manager of the world's greatest resource: CHILDREN!~ Thurgood Marshall

I believe that every human soul is teaching something to someone nearly every minute here in mortality. - M. Russell Ballard

I cannot be a teacher without exposing who I am.
-- Paulo Freire

I cannot teach anybody anything, I can only make them think.
- Socrates

I have been maturing as a teacher. New experiences bring new sensitivities and flexibility. - Howard Lester

I hear and I forget. I see and I remember. I do and I understand. - Chinese Proverb

I know but one freedom and that is the freedom of the mind.
- Antoine de Saint Exupery

I like a teacher who gives you something to take home to think about besides homework. - Lily Tomlin as Edith Ann

*I never teach my pupils. I only attempt to provide the conditions
in which they can learn. ~ Albert Einstein*

I put the relation of a fine teacher to a student just below the relation of a mother to a son. - Thomas Wolfe

I respect faith, but doubt is what gets you an education.
- Wilson Mizner

I would thank you from the bottom of my heart, but for you my
heart has no bottom. ~. John Cotton

I'm not sayin' I'm gonna change the world, but I guarantee that
I will spark the brain that will. - Tupac Shakur

If a child can't learn the way we teach, maybe we should teach the way they learn. - Ignacio 'Nacho' Estrada

If students don't feel teacher appreciation, their whole education has failed. - Michael Balkers

If we teach today's students as we taught yesterday's, we rob them of tomorrow. - John Dewey

If you have knowledge, let others light their candles at it.
~Margaret Fuller

If you judge people, you have no time to love them.
-Mother Teresa

If you think education is expensive, try ignorance.
-   Andy McIntyre

*If you want others to be happy, practice compassion. If you want
to be happy, practice compassion. -Dalai Lama*

If you would thoroughly know anything, teach it to others.
- Tryon Edwards

In teaching you cannot see the fruit of a day's work. It is invisible and remains so, maybe for twenty years. -- Jacques B

In the practical use of our intellect, forgetting is as important as remembering. - William James

Individually, we are one drop. Together we are an ocean.
-   Ryunosuke Satoro

Information is the currency of democracy.
--Ralph Nader

It always seems impossible until it is done.
-Nelson Mandela

It is a luxury to learn; but the luxury of learning is not to be compared with the luxury of teaching. - Roswell D. Hitchcock

It is the supreme art of the teacher to awaken joy in creative expression and knowledge. - Albert Einstein

It's what you learn after you know it all that counts.
-- Harry S. Truman

Knowledge comes, but wisdom lingers.
- Tennyson

Learning is never done without errors and defeat.
- Vladimir Lenin

Learning is not a spectator sport.
- D. Blocher

Let the potential artist in our children come to life that they may surmount industrial monotonies and pressures. - Barbara M

Men learn while they teach.
Lucius A. Seneca

Most people are about as happy as they make up their minds to
be. -Abraham Lincoln

My best friend is the one who brings out the best in me.
- Henry Ford

My country is a country of teachers. It is therefore a country of
peace. -- Oscar Arias Sanchez

Never discourage anyone…who continually makes progress, no matter how slow. - Plato

Nine-tenths of education is encouragement.
- Anatole France

No matter how good teaching may be, each student must take the responsibility for his own education. - John Carolus S.J.

No one can become really educated without having pursued some
study in which he took no interest. - T.S. Eliot

No one who achieves success does so without acknowledging the
help of others. ~John Cotton

Obstacles are those frightful things you see when you take your eyes off your goal. -Henry Ford

Often, when I am reading a good book, I stop and thank my teacher. - Victor Hugo

One good teacher in a lifetime may sometimes change a delinquent into a solid citizen. -- Philip Wylie

One must learn by doing the thing; for though you think you
know it, you have no certainty, until you try. - Sophocles

One of the biggest things that needs to change is the educational system. - Ray C. Anderson

Opportunities are usually disguised as hard work so most people don't recognize them. -Ann Landers

Our progress as a nation can be no swifter than our progress in education. The human mind is a big resource. J. Kennedy

Outside of a dog, a book is man's best friend. Inside of a dog it's too dark to read. -Groucho Marx

People learn more quickly by doing something or seeing something done. - Gilbert Highet

People's behavior makes sense if you think about it in terms of their goals, needs, and motives. - Thomas Mann

Reinventing the wheel is a process.
- Rashid Elisha

Seldom was any knowledge given to keep, but to impart; the grace of this rich jewel is lost in concealment. - Bishop Hall

Spoon feeding in the long run teaches us nothing but the shape of the spoon. - E. M. Forster

When we try to teach our children all about life, our children teach us what life is all about. ~Angela Schwindt

Summer vacation is the time when parents realize that teachers are grossly underpaid. ~John Cotton

Teach the children so that it willnot be necessary to teach the
adults. - Abraham Lincoln

Teacher appreciation makes the world of education go around.
- Helen Peters

Teachers appreciate being appreciated, for teacher appreciation is their highest award. - William Prince

Teachers open the door, but you must enter by yourself.
- Chinese Proverb

You don't choose your family. They are God's gift to you, as you
are to them. ~ Desmond Tutu

Teachers teach because they care. Teaching young people is what they do best. It requires long hours, patience, and care.--Horace

Teachers touch the future.
~John Cotton

Teaching creates all other professions.
~John Cotton

Teaching is not a lost art, but the regard for it is a lost tradition.
-- Jacques Barzun

Teaching is the greatest act of optimism.
- Colleen Wilcox

Your best teacher is your last mistake.
-- Ralph Nader

Manufactured by Amazon.ca
Bolton, ON

16385207R00083